P9-DGI-076

WOULD YOU RATHER...?

TRIPPIN' EDITION

Over 300 Diabolically Deranged Dilemmas to Ponder

Justin Heimberg & David Gomberg

Published by Falls Media
276 Fifth Avenue, Suite 301
New York, NY 10001

First Printing, April 2008
10 9 8 7 6 5 4 3
© Copyright Justin Heimberg and David Gomberg, 2008
All Rights Reserved

Would You Rather...?® is a registered trademark owned by Falls Media

Design by Tom Schirtz

ISBN-13 978-0-9788178-3-1

www.wouldyourather.com / www.falls-media.com

How To Use This Book

Sit around with a bunch of friends and read a question out loud. Discuss the advantages and drawbacks of each option before making a choice. Use your imagination (especially the irreverent, deviant part you normally shy away from) to think of the multitude of ways the choice could affect you. The question is merely a springboard for your conversation.

Everybody must choose. As the Deity proclaims, **YOU MUST CHOOSE!** Once everyone has chosen, move on to the next question. It's that simple.

If you receive a question directed at females, and you are a male (or vice-versa), you can do one of several things: a) move on to another question, b) answer the question anyway, or c) freak out.

Throughout the book, we've laced in lots of non-*Would You Rather...?* travel games that work on the road, though many of them can be played anywhere. The instructions for these games are on their respective pages.

Practice kind randomness and beautiful acts of senselessness.

– Ancient proverb

Special Features of *Trippin' Edition*:

ROADKILL: Occasionally you'll see this icon:  This signifies a game or diversion that you can play which, like a time-killer, will eat up some road on your journey. And like most time-killers, the games are ludicrous, idiotic, and extremely entertaining. (For more games, see the Appendix: "More Roadkill Travel Games".)

QUESTIONS OF CHARACTER:

These questions veer from the standard *Would you rather...?* format. Christ, why would we do that?! Because these questions will give you a sense of what you are all about. Answer these questions and discuss the answers with your friends until things get awkward and uncomfortable. ☺

Table of Contents

Know Your Limit

A Note from the Authors

In case you're retarded, we should explain that the title *Would You Rather...? Trippin' Edition* reeks a bit of double-entendre. In one sense, this is the perfect road trip book: a short, socially interactive book of funny questions ideal for wasting time on a long drive (not to mention, a bunch of humorous travel games and diversions added throughout). Secondly, the over-the-top, trippy, psychedelic tone of many of the questions implies a sort of mental trip. This trip is a journey of self-examination and discovery, a guided meditation of the absurd, which, when followed, leads to a deeper awareness of oneself and the universe. That's right, deliberating whether you'd prefer to fart marbles or cry sap is a modern equivalent of the Zen kōan: "What is the sound of one hand clapping?"

Consider and accept that the *Trippin'* edition is a living roadmap to a deeper consciousness; a consensual journey to a deeper truth. (Or if you prefer, a way to kill two hours in the car or two minutes on the can.) Enjoy.

-'bergs

MILE 1:

THE JOURNEY BEGINS

THESE ARE THE CIRCUMSTANCES. You're in a car, or a van, or a plane, or maybe a stationary, wheel-less car (also known as a room)—on your way somewhere physically or in your own mind or both—when all of the sudden, a powerful Deity materializes out of the ether. He gazes deeply into your eyes, then in your ears, then in your nasal cavity. Upon his examination, the Deity concludes your trip needs a tour guide—someone to prod your soul and mind with questions that, when contemplated, lead to Enlightenment. He initiates his communication. His words are not uttered, but rather, he begins to slobber dialogue bubbles that, like balloons filling with helium, inflate and materialize into visual dilemmas—questions for you and your friends to deliberate. What sort of hallucinogen has the Deity exhaled? you wonder. But there are other questions to answer first...

Would you rather...

never be able to open your mouth when throwing up

OR

have your nostrils and lips seal shut when you sneeze?

Would you rather...

have a sleep disorder that causes you to forcefully shadow box in your sleep

OR

have a penis that, when erect, points to the correct time like the hour hand on a clock?

Things to consider: sleeping next to someone, difficulty of having a sexual relationship, breaking nightstand lamps, 3:30

YOU MUST CHOOSE!

Would you rather...

have sex with Victoria Beckham if she gained 60 pounds

OR

if she lost 20 pounds?

YOU MUST CHOOSE!

Would you rather...

take 900 consecutive punches to the taint by Chuck Norris

OR

have your eyelids pulled taut and cut off by tweezers?

Things to consider: likelihood of survival after taint pummeling, sleeping, bloody tears (for both options), literally having the shit beat out of you

ROADKILL TOLL BOOTH BASKETBALL

Here's a game that can create some road rage in fellow drivers. If you come to an automated toll booth, don't just drop the money in the basket. Instead, try a hook shot over the car from the passenger seat.

Better yet, play Horse with quarters.

YOU MUST CHOOSE!

Would you rather...

remove your two front teeth with a bottle opener

OR

pierce your ears, nose, and navel with a hole-puncher?

YOU MUST CHOOSE!

Would you rather...

have a speech impediment where you switch "f" sounds and "d" sounds

OR

where you switch "c" sounds and "r" sounds?

Things to consider: reading *The Ugly Duckling* to a child, the runt of the litter, playing darts, rock-hard abs, etc.

YOU MUST CHOOSE!

Would you rather...

stutter-r-r-r at-t-t-t the-e-e-e end-d-d-d of-f-f-f every-y-y-y word-d-d-d

OR

have written *fuck!* Tourette's Syndrome *balls!?*

Things to *ass-munch!* consider: power point *dildo!* presentations, love letters *cunttrap!*; *shit-ass!*; *fuck!*; *dickdangle!*

Would you rather...

have an innate gift to infallibly select the fastest moving checkout line

OR

be able to sense farts 30 seconds before they happen (like a Spidey-sense)?

YOU MUST CHOOSE!

Would you rather...

have rusty razor blades hammered beneath each of your fingernails

OR

push your face onto a belt-sander for two minutes?

YOU MUST CHOOSE!

Would you rather...

find out that all of your moments in front of a mirror in the past week have been secretly filmed and broadcast on YouTube

OR

that the last 30 minutes of conversation has been secretly filmed and broadcast on YouTube?

YOU MUST CHOOSE!

Would you rather...

have Wii controls that work for real people in front of you (voodoo style)

OR

have everything you write in Wikipedia become true until the editors fix it?

YOU MUST CHOOSE!

Left, Right, or Center?

Would you rather...

for five dollars, engage in a staring contest with the person on your left (clockwise)

OR

engage in a best three out of five Rock, Paper, Scissors battle with the person to your right (counterclockwise)?

Things to consider: Make it happen.

Would you rather...

dry-hump the person on your left (clockwise)

OR

be manually stimulated by the person to your right (counterclockwise)?

Things to consider: Make it happen?

YOU MUST CHOOSE!

Who would you rather fight to the death...

1 American Gladiator **OR** 10 Hillary Clintons?

1,000 Gumbys **OR** 100 Monchhichis?

12 rabbis with 'roid rage **OR** 44 Mr. Peanuts?

Would you rather...

have a neck as long as your torso

OR

have a torso as short as your neck?
Things to consider: driving (accelerating quickly,
putting phone books on the seat, need for sun roof)

YOU MUST CHOOSE!

Would you rather...

only be able to hear words spoken by females

OR

upon hitting the age of 60, have your psyche slowly devolve into that of a salmon?

Things to consider: impact on friendships, choirs, nagging urge to swim upcurrent

YOU MUST CHOOSE!

Would you rather...

have the *SportsCenter* guys do a full televised recap (complete with highlights and analysis) on ESPN whenever you return from a date

OR

whenever you have a bowel movement?

ROADKILL FILL'ER UP!

Next time you stop for gas, guess how much it will cost to fill the tank. Whoever comes closest doesn't need to contribute to the total bill. Or, whoever's guess is the worst has to pick up the whole tab.

YOU MUST CHOOSE!

Cubicle Conundrums

Would you rather...

have a self-refilling coffee mug that keeps your sugar/cream ratio perfect

OR

have throwing star business cards?

Would you rather...

always type with the maniacal fervor of a mad genius pianist

OR

have an automatic email signature that says "Certified Muff Diver" under your name where your job title goes?

YOU MUST CHOOSE!

Would you rather...

have hair that can harden into a helmet at your command

OR

have universally adaptable Bluetooth speakers built into your ears?

Things to consider: skateboarding; motorcycling; Where's your subwoofer?;
What if the choice was to have pubic hair that could harden into crotch protection?

YOU MUST CHOOSE!

Would you rather...

have sex with the first human image you see when you Google "pelican enthusiast"

OR

the first human image you see when you Google "milky thighs"?

Things to consider: Guess first what you would choose, then Google and decide.

YOU MUST CHOOSE!

THE GOOGLE GAME — ROADKILL

Open up Google on your computer or mobile phone. The object of the game is to get the desired topic to show up on the first web page (showing up anywhere without have to click). The catch is you cannot use the most obvious words or the topic itself.

You may enter any other 3 words into the search bar.

Topic	Forbidden Words
Ronald Reagan	President, US, Iran/Contra, Republican, George Bush, Politics, 80's
Pamela Anderson	Tommy Lee, Baywatch, VIP, sex tape, Playboy, breasts, Home Improvement
69	Sex, positions, oral sex, asparagus, The Three Stooges, Ken Singleton, mulch

ROADKILL CAR BINGO

Divide into two teams. Each team picks a Bingo page.
Each time you spot one of the items below, mark the box.

Person giving the finger	Someone singing to themselves in a car	Drunk person on street
Jaywalker	Doobie Brothers song on radio	Nose-picker
Asshole who cuts you off	Religious zealot bumper sticker	Roadkill—deer, fox, or pelican

Card 1

The first team to mark three boxes in a row, horizontally, vertically, or diagonally wins. Or if you're not into the whole competition thing, work together.

Obese person eating in car	Graffiti with a misspelling	Audible fart
Mustard	Guy driving who thinks he is cooler than he actually is	Fuzzy Dice
Vanity license plate with sexual content	Guilt	Roadkill—squirrel, possum, or Ewok

MILE 10:

THE JOURNEY CONTINUES

As your surroundings rush by, things are getting blurry, less-fixed, wavering. The world is a bad cable connection. The Deity's fro-tee appears as smoke—or is it the rushing tides?—Poseidon, Hades, and Gabe Kaplan photo-morphed together. His enticing interrogation continues; but the Deity no longer communicates with you by dialogue bubbles. Instead, implementing numerous bottles of sodas and seltzers, he uses a language consisting of spilling that, in your budding state of understanding, you somehow comprehend.

As always, you must choose ...

Would you rather...

have a bad acid trip in Amish Country **OR** in Bed Bath & Beyond?

in Home Depot **OR** in the library?

while watching *Teletubbies* **OR** *Deal or No Deal*?

YOU MUST CHOOSE!

Would you rather...

be able to delete memories in your mind as if they were files on a computer

OR

be able to network to other people's brains so you could share knowledge (provided they agreed to give you access)?

ROADKILL YOU BET

Guess the number of miles on car speedometers as you pass (this requires you to roll down your window at high speed to ask the driver the answer). Choose a wager amount. Whoever is closest wins the wager.

YOU MUST CHOOSE!

Would you rather...

suck in air with the force of a vacuum when yawning

OR

have blow-dryer strength flatulence?

Would you rather...

have red-eye in real life

OR

at cocktail/dinner parties, become incorrigibly convinced you are working at a 1920s meatpacking factory?

Things to consider: corporate barbeques, wedding reception home movies

YOU MUST CHOOSE!

Taking Things Literally

Would you rather...

have diarrhea of the mouth, literally **OR** have legs of Jello, literally?

have a magnetic personality, literally **OR** a cute button nose, literally?

have puppy-dog eyes, literally, **OR** have a nonfunctional Timothy Busfield's head protruding from your hip, literally?

YOU MUST CHOOSE!

Would you rather...

have everything you say have an interrogative inflection?

OR

your have the random sentence words in out come order?

YOU MUST CHOOSE!

Would you rather...

have a two-inch underbite

OR

a two-inch overbite? Sidebite?

YOU MUST CHOOSE!

Would you rather...

have finite amounts of emotions (e.g., resentment, sadness, happiness) like various color printer ink cartridges

OR

as you drink, become incredibly adamant about the superiority of isosceles triangles to the point of starting fights?

Things to consider: *Scalene?!* Are you freakin' kidding me?!

YOU MUST CHOOSE!

Would you rather...

BE A TRANSFORMER WHO CAN CHANGE INTO A GEORGE FOREMAN GRILL

OR

A YARMULKE?

YOU MUST CHOOSE!

Would you rather...

have permanent Milwaukee's Best aftertaste

OR

have a muscular palsy where you always walk as if you're laying down a bunt?

Would you rather...

use dry ice deodorant once a day

OR

sulfuric acid spray perfume/cologne?

YOU MUST CHOOSE!

Would you rather...

have a bipolar disorder where your mood wildly swings every four seconds from extremely manic to extremely depressed

OR

have a multiple personality disorder consisting of the following personalities: surly dockworker, pompous cobbler, and a seven year old who is nervous about his piñata-striking abilities?

ROADKILL SPIT TAKE

The "laughers" of the group each take a big swig of a beverage just as someone reads a question in the book or offers some of their own comedy stylings.
The goal is to get someone to laugh while drinking and give the perfect "spit take".

YOU MUST CHOOSE!

Would you rather...

only become sexually excited while watching *Inside the Actor's Studio*

OR

be limited to having sexual relations with people dressed as characters from *Charlie Brown*?

Things to consider: matching the orgasmic appreciation of James Lipton, learning how to smoothly say "Here, try this on."

YOU MUST CHOOSE!

Would you rather...

only be able to open your eyes 1/8 of an inch

OR

only be able to open your mouth 1/8 of an inch?
Things to consider: eating, bad karaoke, unintentional leering

YOU MUST CHOOSE!

Would you rather...

have a type of anorexia where the left side of your body appears incredibly fat to you

OR

have a severe phobia of 47 degree angles?

Things to consider: How would you dress?, brief moments of panic during see-saw play, geometry class

Would you rather...

have a nice timbre to your voice but always be trying to figure out which way the wind is blowing

OR

cultivate a sense of gravitas but compulsively hit yourself in the crotch with great force every ten minutes?

YOU MUST CHOOSE!

Would you rather...

be able to italicize printed lettering by sheer force of will and a concentrated stare

OR

be able to spit tartar sauce?

Would you rather...

have your body marbled with Asiago cheese

OR

have breasts that inflate and deflate with your breath like a frog's throat?

Things to consider: elastic bras, love life, sleeping

YOU MUST CHOOSE!

Would you rather...

have your tonsils removed with a fork and steak knife

OR

place your ankles on a train track and let them be run over by Amtrak's Acela Express?

YOU MUST CHOOSE!

Would you rather...

have to ride a hop ball to work/school each day

OR

subsist solely on any free samples you can score at supermarkets?
Things to consider: the feeling of being a fraud by constantly feigning interest in buying samples

YOU MUST CHOOSE!

Look at a car ahead of you. Guess what the person will look like based on their car. Include race, age, and sex. Be specific. For example, if you see a Volvo up ahead, you might say, "a middle-aged mom who's lost any sense of her sexuality", while another passenger might say "a hipster with horn-rimmed glasses." If you see a low-rider, you could guess "a bad-ass vato gang member" or "a redneck teenager smoking." Speed up (safely), get next to the car and look (safely) and see who is closest. Repeat (safely). First one to five points wins (safely).

Authors are not responsible for bad or irresponsible driving.

REst Stop

PIMP YOUR RIDE

Just as your body is but a casing of your energy, your car is a vessel of your group's energy. (If it helps, picture your car with a skin paint job and veiny upholstery). A vessel is vital in the manifestation of one's aura, and thusly should be tended to and made holy. And so for better or for worse depending on his mood, the Deity feels it is time to take a break from affecting your journey to examine and change the means by which you take it. In other words, he's going to make-over your wheels and give a little of his own Driver's Ed to make your travels more interesting.

Would you rather...

have to always drive on highways "playing Pac-Man"—where your car straddles the dotted white lines that divide lanes

OR

have to drive with your seat at a 45 degree angle forward? 150 degree backward? Turned 90 degrees to the right?

Things to consider: For entertainment purposes only. Do not try this.

YOU MUST CHOOSE!

Would you rather...

have strobe light headlights

OR

have to arm wrestle an increasingly strong gearshift to get into the next gear?

Would you rather...

have a horn that can project a hologram of a big middle finger

OR

your car alarm-beep sound be the *Law & Order* sound?
Things to consider: inadvertent summoning of Sam Waterston

YOU MUST CHOOSE!

43

Would you rather...

have a car whose paint job features a giant face of Alan Greenspan on the hood like the firebird on a Trans Am

OR

a car with a "Rico Suave" cassingle stuck in the tape deck?

ROADKILL SIR MIXES-FAIRLY-OFTEN

Have a contest to see who can make the worst playlist of songs. The winner gets his list played and gets to listen to a separate iPod (with earphones) while others in the car must endure it.

YOU MUST CHOOSE!

Would you rather...

be immune from speeding laws

OR

be immune to paranoid, borderline-racist instincts to hit the electronic door locks when driving through poorer neighborhoods?

Things to consider: Justin is so cowardly that he actually once hit the locks on instinct when he saw a scary dog in the next car.

YOU MUST CHOOSE!

Would you rather...

have to drive to the rhythm of whatever song is on the radio

OR

have to pick up every hitchhiker you ever see and beat them in a game of "20 Questions" before you can drop them off?

YOU MUST CHOOSE!

Would you rather...

have to always drive twice the speed limit

OR

always drive half the speed limit?
What if it were 1/3 the speed limit?

YOU MUST CHOOSE!

MILE 30:

TRAVELLING DEEPER

Inward and onward you venture. Perhaps the Twinkees the Deity gave you had more in them than high fructose corn syrup. You stare into your navel and see infinity. As you pluck your gaze from the endless depths of your belly-button, you discover that your friends' heads have been replaced with those of the cast of the Brady Bunch. Weirder still, you find yourself oddly attracted to Florence Henderson. Profundities pop up in your mind like brain acne and you realize that "question" begins with "quest." And the questions continue, but to reach you, the Deity no longer uses dialogue bubbles, nor his spilling language, but he now communicates through odor, a "smelody" - a modulating continuum (one pole Rose, the other Pickle) that somehow you understand — Yes, you are starting to understand more and more as you contemplate his questions...

Ten minutes before your death, would you rather find out...

there is no God

OR

that this whole time the term "au jus" translated to "ass juice"?

YOU MUST CHOOSE!

Would you rather...

have to plug yourself in every few hours to recharge before you shut down like a laptop

OR

only be able to travel by means of rickshaw?
Things to consider: camping trips; car adapters

YOU MUST CHOOSE!

Would you rather...

die by having kazoos shoved down your mouth until you suffocate

OR

die by panda mauling and possible rape?

Things to consider: the sound of your last gasps; panda's cuteness a mitigating factor?

YOU MUST CHOOSE!

BATTLE HAIKU ROADKILL

Here's how this works: Two people engage in Battle Haiku, where they insult each other à la Battle Rap. But instead of rap, use the lost art of Japanese Haiku poetry. The poems must insult the opponent in a good-natured way and follow a syllable pattern of 5-7-5. Invoking nature is encouraged. Examples follow.

You have ugly teeth
Smile looks like wilting lotus
Crapped on by hawk

Well, you are so fat
Flesh is like cumulus cloud
Drifting in the wind.

Damn, yo!

Would you rather...

have no joints

OR

thirteen anuses?

Things to consider: Plinko-like digestive track; guessing which anus will be the point of excretion, and is there a casino game in that?

Let us know!
How did each of you envision the 13 anuses?
Where and in what pattern?
Email your answers to anusarrangement@wouldyourather.com

YOU MUST CHOOSE!

Would you rather...

permanently share your bedroom with 1,000 mosquitoes **OR** 5 boa constrictors?

25 black widow spiders **OR** 3 landmines?

The ghost of Frederick Douglass **OR** heavy metal band Pantera?

Four Aleksandr Pushkin imitators **OR** "Leaping" Lanny Poffo in his prime? (Google them.)

YOU MUST CHOOSE!

TechZone 2000

Would you rather...

never receive another piece of email spam

OR

learn that all the spam you receive is actually 100 percent true?

Things to consider: constant willing sex partners who are often bored; those poor suffering people from Africa with interesting syntax; ability to add inches to your penis until your penis surpasses 10 feet in length

YOU MUST CHOOSE!

Would you rather...

be able to "flag" people like you can with email senders, so that a force-field would automatically keep them out of your sight

OR

be able to "re-skin" your lover at-will as you would an online avatar?

Things to consider: Who would you "flag"? What would you "re-skin" your lover as?

QUESTION of CHARACTER:

If you could live in the world of one video game, what would you choose?
Halo? Madden? Q-bert?

YOU MUST CHOOSE!

You must do one of the following, or the Deity will kill your family.

Would you rather...

cough "Boring!" during a wedding ceremony of a close relative

OR

wear an oversized hockey jersey and one of those foam "Number 1" hands to the funeral of a family friend?

During a business meeting, would you rather...

have to use the phrase "cumload" four times

OR

have to wear those blue and red 3D glasses for the entire meeting?

Things to consider: Subtly injecting the profanity in corporate context: "We had a cumload of response from our new marketing campaign"; "Let's be proactive and get a cumload of buzz going"; "Marsha, is that a cumload on your shirt?"

YOU MUST CHOOSE!

Would you rather...

have a pimento permanently housed in each nostril

OR

have hairy teeth and gums?

Things to consider: gum stubble; flossing; the pimento lobby (Big Pimento)

Let us know:
Do pimentos have any uses other than olive filling?
If you know of one, send an email to
pimentouse@wouldyourather.com.

YOU MUST CHOOSE!

Would you rather...

have the power to "bookmark" places you've been and be able to return to those places by simply snapping your fingers

OR

be able to travel by conceptual hyperlink (teleport based on topic associations to what you see)?

YOU MUST CHOOSE!

Would you rather...

have to use every page in this book as toilet paper

OR

have to smoke every page in this book?

ROADKILL ALMOST FAMOUS

Pick random people you see and say the celebrity they look most like. Say something every time. The comedy comes from how much of a stretch it is.

YOU MUST CHOOSE!

Would you rather...

have a delusional paranoia where you reflexively try to perform CPR whenever you see anyone sleeping

OR

have farts that release explosive red dye similar to the dye packs found in bags of money during bank robberies?

Things to consider: worried launderers; resuscitation attempts being mistaken for sexual advances; someone dozing off on the subway

YOU MUST CHOOSE!

Would you rather...

see how many grapes you can fit in your mouth at once

OR

how many almonds you can fit in your nose?

Things to consider: We would never suggest you do something so entertaining and dangerous and disclaim any liability for you doing anything other than thinking of this in the hypothetical. We also hypothetically recommend smokehouse mesquite almonds.

YOU MUST CHOOSE!

Would you rather have a tattoo of...

an illusion of knee-high tube socks **OR** an illusion of chest hair?

a large back tattoo of the Atari 2600 game *Breakout* **OR** the text of the Magna Carta?

a "tramp stamp" **OR** "taint paint"?

YOU MUST CHOOSE!

Would you rather...

have the power to produce hair gel from your fingertips

OR

be able to donate blood directly through your skin via osmosis?

Would you rather...

be cursed so that all your dry-cleaned shirts are returned to you as Don Drysdale #53 replica jerseys

OR

have a speech disorder where you invariably start every sentence with the phrase "Rumor has it..."?

YOU MUST CHOOSE!

Would you rather...

have all your eye blinks last 10 seconds

OR

have the voice in your head periodically crisscrossed with the line of a telemarketer in Beijing?

Things to consider: test-taking; learning Mandarin; driving

YOU MUST CHOOSE!

The Deity has decided you need to stick up for yourself and be more of a disciplinarian.

Would you rather...

fire a basketball as hard as possible into your mom's face every time she had an irrational worry

OR

taser your child every time he/she whined?

YOU MUST CHOOSE!

Would you rather...

have a minor autism where you are perfectly normal save the propensity to forego shaking hands and instead do that interlocking finger thing where you look and it looks like a butthole

OR

have bee-bee boogers?

Things to consider: Bee-Bee Boogers is:
   a) The worst name ever for porn star?
   b) A legendary Sioux Indian Chieftain?
   c) A gifted blues musician?
   d) Make up your own.

YOU MUST CHOOSE!

Whoever is reading must convey the words below using charades. But here's the catch. You can only use your body from the neck up (i.e., your face).

- Disgusting
- Cross-eyed
- Drunk
- Horny
- Cunnilingus
- Pink Eye
- William H. Macy
- Supercilious

Team 1

Would You Rather...? TRIPPIN' EDITION

See how many you can get in three minutes. If you'd like, split into teams. Each time you use a part of your body other than your face, deduct one point. Winner gets the next food stop paid for.

Team 2

- Excited
- Death
- Worry
- Gum
- Sexy
- Spit
- Vomit
- Vasco da Gama

A Sex CHAPTER?

This book, this quest, is about more than superficial carnal needs. For questions regarding the flesh, there is, after all, *Would You Rather...? Love & Sex* available at wouldyourather.com for $9.95. But this book and this journey transcend the Self and its basest needs. Trips like this one are about something greater than the ego; they concern one's connection to the Great Around. They are part of a spiritual revolution. Wait a second. The Deity *is* telling us something. Oh. Well, it turns out every spiritual or social movement in history was really just a bunch of people trying to get laid. The hippie movement of the sixties, women's lib, and don't even get us started about the Protestant Reformation (Orgy City!). And so, in that great tradition of bullshit social/spiritual movements that are actually veiled attempts at getting some action, the Deity gives in and proffers questions to loosen up the mind, libido, and labia.

Would you rather have sex with...

Reese Witherspoon **OR** Jennifer Garner?

Carrie Underwood **OR** *Top Chef*'s Padma Lakshmi?
Things to consider: Salman Rushdie tapped that.

Crazy, chunky Britney circa 2008 **OR** sane, nubile Britney circa 2003?

Paula Abdul **OR** Megan Fox if she were missing an arm? A leg?
An eye? Missing all of the above?

YOU MUST CHOOSE!

Would you rather...

have a sexual partner who talks to you like a motivational speaker during sex

OR

who talks to you like a "bad cop" interrogator?

QUESTION of CHARACTER:

If you had to have one of your sexual encounters leak onto the Internet as a sex tape, which would you choose?

YOU MUST CHOOSE!

Would you rather...

have Internet chat sex (including video of faces but with no volume) with someone who is hot as hell but is just an egregiously awful speller

OR

someone who is decent looking and has great writing panache and grammar skills?

Things to consider: I wunt to nale you. I am masterbating to a clymacks. Are you into annul?

YOU MUST CHOOSE!

Would you rather...

have sex with someone who has the butt of Kim Kardashian and the face of Kim Jong Il

OR

the body of Halle Berry and the head of Frankenberry?

YOU MUST CHOOSE!

Would you rather...

have sex with David Hasselhoff

OR

Johnny Depp if he put on 75 pounds for a movie role?

YOU MUST CHOOSE!

Would you rather have sex with...

Donald Trump **OR** Vince McMahon?

Topher Grace **OR** LeBron James?

Seth Rogen **OR** Mario Lopez?

Dennis Kucinich if he had a 10-inch penis **OR** John Edwards if he had a 3-inch penis?

YOU MUST CHOOSE!

Would you rather...

get to second base with Jessica Simpson

OR

go all the way with Tara Reid?

Would you rather...

get to first base with Angelina Jolie

OR

third base with Helen Hunt?

Would you rather...

get hit by a pitch with Monica Bellucci

OR

foul off a couple close ones and then strike out looking with Briana Banks?

YOU MUST CHOOSE!

Would you rather...

be able to change one physical attribute of your spouse with that change having the opposite effect on you (i.e., the larger you make her breasts, the more concave yours become)

OR

be able to do the same thing but with a mental trait?

Things to consider: What trait would you choose?

YOU MUST CHOOSE!

Would you rather...

have your pubic hair connected to your nose hair

OR

have barbed wire pubic hair?

Things to consider: sex life, beach life, constantly putting your hand in front of your face in feigned concentration

Would you rather...

be able to orgasm without releasing any fluid

OR

be able to instantly turn on and off your erection by clapping?

*Women read this questions as "have a lover who is able to..."

YOU MUST CHOOSE!

Would you rather...

have access to a MySpace-like online community where it was revealed who everyone has had sex with and who their partners have had sex with, and so on

OR

have a TiVo that magically records everything that goes through your partner's head during sex?

YOU MUST CHOOSE!

Would you rather...

have a Jenna Jameson vaginal replica

OR

a Real Doll crafted in the spitting image of Louisa May Alcott?

YOU MUST CHOOSE!

Super Couples

The Deity loves Celebrity Couples, whether real or of his own concoction. He also likes to throw you into the mix.

Would you rather have sex with...

Brangelina (Brad Pitt and Angelina Jolie) or Romotional Strategy (Tony Romo and Jessica Simpson)?

Albacore (Jessica Alba and Corey Feldman) **OR** Katfish (Kat Von D and Laurence Fishburne)?

Rosebud (Rosie O'Donnell and Bud Bundy—David Faustino) **OR** Windex (Oprah Winfrey and Dexter Manley)?

YOU MUST CHOOSE!

THE PORTMANTEAU GAME

A "portmanteau word" is when you combine two words to make one like "brunch" or the celebrity super couples on the last page. Try your hand coming up with your own hypothetical Hollywood super couples. Example: Snoop Dogg + Carrie Underwood = Underdogg.

Warm up with this quiz.

Bob Saget + Katherine Heigl = ?

Dr. Phil + Hillary Duff = ?

Natalie Portman + Tony Danza = ?

Answers: Bobkat; Phillary; Portmanteau

NONSTANDARD DEVIATION

Which are real names for deviant sexual maneuvers and which are fake?

Arabian Goggles (testicles settle in eye sockets)

Viking Funeral (a woman's manual stimulation of two phalluses above her head)

Cleveland Steamer (feces is laid upon chest for erotic purposes)

A Poor Man's Walrus (double nasal penetration)

Answers: Arabian Goggles and Cleveland Steamer are real.

Would you rather...

only be able to have low-passion, obligatory "trying to get pregnant" sex

OR

kinky over-the-top bondage/fetish sex with you as the submissive?

Would you rather...

have to drive with only your nondominant hand for the rest of your life

OR

have to pleasure yourself with only your nondominant hand?

YOU MUST CHOOSE!

Would you rather...

have your mom watch a video compilation of all your romantic and sexual moments

OR

vice versa? Same question with your grandma?
Same with Tom Sizemore? Same with Tommy Lasorda?

YOU MUST CHOOSE!

ROADKILL TWO TRUTHS AND A LIE

Each person shares 3 one- or two-sentence stories about themselves, two of which are true. Then, the others guess which is the lie. Here's an example from the authors.

• A model dating a seven-footer was impressed with the use of seven-footers in our books and set Gomberg up on a date with another model.

• Two friends solicited Heimberg via email and he made a tour to "visit" each of them. They asked that they some day be mentioned in one of the books.

• Gomberg hooked up with a professional Cyndi Lauper look-alike.

To find out which is a lie, email: twotruthsonelie@wouldyourather.com.

BAD TRIP

Uh oh, something's going wrong. Those flowers seem to be hissing and that rearview mirror wants to eat your baby. You just got detoured through Enlightenment Adjacent, past Crazytown, and now you're heading into Paranoid City. The Deity's stoic face suddenly looks wrathful. His goatee is made up of snarling snakes and poisonous pipe cleaners. What is happening!? Horrible images flood your mind. What is real and what isn't?

Either way, you need to make a choice fast —

Would you rather have a hallucination of...

your parents melting **OR** your parents having sex?

your own death **OR** John Madden bathing?

being attacked by staplers **OR** being attacked by a swarm of Post-it notes?

YOU MUST CHOOSE!

Would you rather...

eat a sushi roll of maggot-encrusted dorm-bathroom drain clog

OR

sashimi-style sushi consisting of ants carrying a dismembered thumb?

Would you rather...

gargle quick-drying cement mouthwash

OR

inhale Krazy Glue nasal spray?

YOU MUST CHOOSE!

Would you rather...

have live centipedes for arm hair

OR

have your irises/pupils Whited-Out?

YOU MUST CHOOSE!

Would you rather...

fight to the death 2,000 lobsters **OR** one giant Grover?

a rabid Clifford the Big Red Dog **OR** 90 Flat Stanleys?

a rhino **OR** all 43 Presidents of the USA?

ROADKILL WHO WOULD WIN?

This game is a variation of the above. You think of any two things or groups of things and decide who would win in a fight to the death. Examples: Baker vs. Butcher. One hundred bees vs. one squirrel. Five Katie Courics vs. one Stone Cold Steve Austin.

YOU MUST CHOOSE!

Would you rather...

have an impulse control problem that causes you to perform 10 wild pelvic thrusts every hour, on the hour

OR

be unable to refrain from "sacking" the elderly as soon as you see them?

Things to consider: business presentations; going to a retirement home

YOU MUST CHOOSE!

Would you rather have a hallucination of...

the snack you are eating turning to eyeballs **OR** your palm lines becoming worms?

being followed by Charles Grodin **OR** being dry-humped by two koala bears?

John Voight setting up a badminton net **OR** Don Cheadle relaxing on a bench reading the paper?

YOU MUST CHOOSE!

Would you rather...

die by defenestration

OR

by fenestration?

YOU MUST CHOOSE!

Would you rather have a paranoid delusion that...

your shadow is trying to kill you **OR** your tongue is?

your mole is a laser sighting from a gun **OR** your jewelry is constricting you?

that your significant other is having an affair **OR** that your best friend is a Yeti?

YOU MUST CHOOSE!

Which evil voice would you rather have stuck in your head...

Simon Cowell belittling you **OR** Paula Abdul being overdramatic?

Chris Collinsworth gainsaying your professional sports team **OR** Diddy being himself?

Drunk Joe Namath coming on to you **OR** drunk Joe Namath coming on you?

A bad Borat impersonator trying to amuse you **OR** the guy from *Police Academy* who makes the crazy sounds trying to scare you?

YOU MUST CHOOSE!

MILE 40:

STEPPING STONES TO NIRVANA

As you continue your journey, your senses begin to intermingle. You can smell concepts, *hear percepts, feel* biceps. Your mind at once becomes clear and murky, *reductionist, holistic;* the world now a pointillist painting of colored dust being scattered by the breath of the ambivalent moon. Sheeyit. You look at your *trippin' friends. They are* all connected with you... by eyelash. A tangled lash-knot is centered between you, *revolving as a metaphor beckoning you to untangle your ego's vision—to see as one humanity. The* hair-nexus begins to grow, a writhing Brillo pad *of communal eyelash* until it takes shape as the Deity's Jew-fro, his face unrolling beneath it. As you stare into the eyes of the hovering head, you sense you are close to enlightenment; *so close that you can* taste it. It tastes like orange sherbet. The Deity's line of inquiry *is getting even more random* and yet you sense purpose—you see his challenge *as suspended* stepping stones to Nirvana over a canyon of deadly Slinkys

Would you rather...

have an inch of flimsy extra skin at the end of your fingers like gloves that are too big

OR

react like a crying, screaming teenage girl seeing the Beatles for the first time whenever you are introduced to a new person?

YOU MUST CHOOSE!

Note: The following question has been paraphrased from Immanuel Kant's *Groundwork of the Metaphysics of Morals*.

Would you rather...

have your feces undulate and ooze like in a lava lamp upon falling in the toilet

OR

be able to fart Morse Code?

Things to consider: rainy days; secretly relaying the truth if captured and filmed by terrorists; --...-.-..--

YOU MUST CHOOSE!

Would you rather...

have a restless leg and a lazy eye

OR

a lazy leg and a restless eye?

Things to consider: Why do they call it a "lazy eye"? That seems pretty cruel and unfair to the eye. It's not lazy. It's trying its best; it just can't quite get the job done. (Note: Go back in time to 1983. Sell joke to Seinfeld.)

YOU MUST CHOOSE!

FASHION INWARD

Sure, you're on a trip to a higher consciousness. But are you dressed for it?

Would you rather...

have to wear clothes five sizes too small

OR

have to wear articles of clothing on a different part of the body than they were intended for?

Things to consider: pants for shirt; socks for gloves; hat for pants; underwear for ascot

YOU MUST CHOOSE!

Would you rather...

have to wear all of your clothing inside out

OR

have to use an immortal flounder for a wallet?

Things to consider: important business lunches where you pick up the check, dropping your fish, "Immortal Flounder" = good band name

YOU MUST CHOOSE!

Would you rather always have to wear...

clothes in the style of an 8 year old **OR** an 80 year old?

a full Georgetown Hoya uniform **OR** an eye patch?

pleather **OR** highly fashionable outfits except that the shirts all have holes cut out at the nipples?

 **ROADKILL SHAREWEAR**

Stop at a thrift store or, if none is near, a Kmart or something. Each passenger gets $20 to buy clothing for another person. The person you buy clothes for has to where whatever you bought later that night in public.

YOU MUST CHOOSE!

109

Would you rather...

be judged by *Project Runway*'s fashion judges as you leave for work each day

OR

have all your meals critiqued by *Top Chef* judges?

Things to consider: Michael Kors = Fat Anthony Michael Hall; Tom Colicchio = Fat Cal Ripken, Jr. (Google them.)

QUESTION of CHARACTER:

*If you could watch any reality show where
people competed at anything and were judged
in overdramatic and critical ways, what would
you choose as the competition?*

YOU MUST CHOOSE!

Would you rather...

be incapable of seeing or hearing people over the age of 40

OR

under the age of 20?

Things to consider: marriage; kids; quiet plane rides

YOU MUST CHOOSE!

Would you rather...

only be able to travel downhill for the rest of your life (you get to first move anywhere you want)

OR

only be able to speak with words in alphabetical order
(each ensuing word must come later alphabetically than the one before it)?

Look up about an inch. See that second option? Give it a try for as long as you can. Try to really communicate with the restriction.

YOU MUST CHOOSE!

Not-So-Super Powers

In your altered state, the Deity offers you the chance to possess a power. You are a golden god! Actually, maybe it's closer to bronze.

Would you rather...

be able to cool coffee to a perfect drinkable temperature with merely one blow

OR

be able to neaten sloppy joes?

Things to consider: career options

YOU MUST CHOOSE!

Would you rather...

be able to inflate your muscles to look strong but have no actual exceptional strength

OR

be extremely strong, but have the body of this guy...

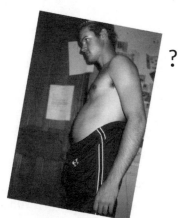

?

YOU MUST CHOOSE!

You say Pimento, I also say Pimento.

By popular demand, here are more pimento questions. You can all stop with the letters now!

Would you rather...

have telekinetic powers restricted to moving pimento

OR

be able to see through pimento?
Things to consider: olive factory work

Would you rather...

live in a world where it rained pimento

OR

name your first born "Pimento"?
Things to consider: feeding starving nations with the ample supply of pimento; "Pim" for short

YOU MUST CHOOSE!

Would you rather...

be able to do a perfect rendition of Nena's "99 Red Balloons" by cracking your knuckles

OR

be able to perform a masterfully timed routine of Abbott and Costello's "Who's on First?" in sign language?

Would you rather...

be incredibly charming from 3:32 p.m. to 3:35 p.m. every day

OR

have a bionic arm but be a compulsive masturbator?

Things to consider: first dates starting promptly at 3:32; the sound of your bionic motion as you near orgasm

YOU MUST CHOOSE!

Would you rather...

your farts be literally silent but deadly

OR

be audible and capable of inducing second degree burns?

Would you rather...

be able to legally notarize documents by biting down on them

OR

be able to bolster the confidence of Arby's workers?

YOU MUST CHOOSE!

Would you rather...

be able to fly one inch off the ground

OR

be able to project invisible lukewarm ray beams from your eyes?

YOU MUST CHOOSE!

Would you rather...

be able to highlight print with your finger

OR

be able to induce nosebleeds to people on live TV?

Things to consider: political debates; news anchors; NBA free throws

Would you rather...

play a game of paintball with the Dalai Lama

OR

play 20 Questions with Shannon Sharpe?

YOU MUST CHOOSE!

ROADKILL CAR RADIO BINGO

Divide into two teams. Each team picks a Bingo page. Take
turns, two minutes each, fiddling with the radio, listening for

Beatles song	The word "Jesus"	The phrase "partly cloudy"
A rant	An undeniably annoying commercial	A guitar solo
The word "foot"	Crying	Simon Bolivar impersonator

Card 1

any of the items in the charts below. Each time you spot one of the items below, mark the box. The first team to mark three boxes in a row, horizontally, vertically, or diagonally wins. Or if you're not into the whole competition thing, work together.

The word "love"	Laughter	A siren
Static	A moronic opinion	A cheesy sound effect from a DJ
A lyric glorifying violence	A lyric glorifying bad treatment of women	A lyric glorifying gnomes

Card 2 (if necessary, tear this page out. Take it to the Man!)

REst Stop

The past few miles have been a **blur—literally**, *as you believe you were traveling* at a speed of roughly *400 miles per hour. The last* thing you remember was when the cop pulled *you over, you* calmly explained you were speeding "to avoid the dragon." That was two days ago. As you come to, you see on the seat next to you: a lasso, an oven mitt, a pack of Rolaids, and a bloody Menorah. Better get rid of those. You pull up to a rest stop. Perfect, because you're hungry. You approach an **unusual vend-ing machine**, where each selection must be made as a choice between two items.

Would you rather...

drink a Big Gulp of sweat wrung from WNBA players' undergarments

OR

a bowl of ice-cold saliva topped with floss residue collected over 10 years from British homeless men's teeth?

YOU MUST CHOOSE!

Would you rather...

use silverware that consists of unwashed surgical instruments recently used in an open heart surgery operation

OR

use a straw that was cut from unwashed tubing used in a liposuction procedure?

Would you rather...

drink a cappuccino topped with whipped rabid-St. Bernard slobber froth

OR

iced tea sweetened with a spoonful of vaginal discharge from a VH1's *Rock of Love* with Bret Michaels contestant?

Things to consider: getting infected

YOU MUST CHOOSE!

Would you rather...

have a scoop of vanilla ice cream encrusted with pubic hair trimmings

OR

a steaming slice of apple pie warmed with the flatulence of 1,000 chili-eating beer drinkers?

ROADKILL GUESS THAT HAIR

Here's a game, courtesy of Mr. Jason Penfield Heimberg, brother of author Justin. Everybody closes or diverts their eyes (except the driver), as one person plucks a hair from any part of the body. The hair is then passed around. Everybody guesses what part of the body the hair came from. Winner gets control of the music for the next 10 minutes (and gets to keep the hair).

YOU MUST CHOOSE!

Would you rather...

have a bowl of tapeworm "linguini"

OR

a slice of pizza topped with recently-pulled-teeth "pine nuts" and dried-scab "pepperoni"?

Would you rather...

consume 800 Twizzlers in 10 minutes

OR

4,000 Peanut M&M's?

YOU MUST CHOOSE!

Would you rather...

eat a stick of cotton candy entirely made from belly lint

OR

suck on a human eyeball Jawbreaker for 10 minutes?

Would you rather...

drink a mug of bull semen

OR

a mug of "Bull" semen (as in "Bull" from Night Court)?

Things to consider: the curse of the female bailiff; Harry Anderson: Whereabouts? Anybody?

YOU MUST CHOOSE!

FUN WITH MICROWAVES!

Stop at a 7-Eleven. One person purchases 15 different types of candy (or candy bars) and breaks them into pieces, placing them on individual paper plates. Crank up the 7-Eleven microwave until the candy is thoroughly melted and unidentifiable. Bring the plates to the car. Players then consume the candy, each guessing what they're eating. Obviously, someone will need to have the answers. Feel free to play this game with other edible substances or to mix things together and try to discern the different ingredients.

DEATH SCHMEATH

One cannot truly live without first facing one's death. One cannot be immortal without first accepting one's mortality. One cannot bring in da noise without bringin' in da funk. Such is the life-death paradox. The Deity wears the letters L-I-F-E in brass knuckle rings on the fingers of his left hand and D-E-A-T-H on the fingers of his right hand (yeah, he has an extra). And with his fists, he communicates his questions of pain, torture and death into your soul. A beautiful, brutal pummeling into a delirious bliss. Each bruise is a gift, each shattered rib an insight. You are being jumped into the gang of the Collective Unconscious. Your 40oz. of divine nectar awaits...

Would you rather...

play 30 minutes of continuous dodgeball against Peyton Manning

OR

have a five minute slap fight with Roy Jones, Jr.?

Things to consider: A third option: Suffer through a two hour PowerPoint presentation about how Tom Brady is a superior human to you

Would you rather...

be operated on by the cast (the actors, not the doctors in the show) of *House*

OR

the cast of *Grey's Anatomy*?

YOU MUST CHOOSE!

Would you rather be hunted down by...

Alien **OR** Predator?

Freddie Kruger **OR** Boba Fett?

An evil version or yourself **OR** an evil version of
George Washington Carver?
Things to consider: peanut guns

YOU MUST CHOOSE!

Would you rather...

have your tongue be twisted 720 degrees

OR

have your septum torn out with a staple remover?

Would you rather...

be pelted to death with lettuce heads by a cackling Matt Lauer

OR

be sifted to death?

Things to consider: percentage of population who enjoyed this question: four

YOU MUST CHOOSE!

Which of the following foreign slurs would you rather endure...

Alaka shaza bazil lut kaz! (which means "May a hundred paper cuts incise your testicles!")

OR

Nala frafala matu netala! (which means "May one defecate on your mustache area.")?

Would you rather...

slowly insert a three-inch needle directly into your navel

OR

have to stand on a fired-up BBQ grill for one minute?

YOU MUST CHOOSE!

Would you rather...

have to wash your face every day in a heavily populated birdbath

OR

have to use the piece of toilet paper from the person who last used the toilet?

Things to consider: That makes doo-doo reference #35 in this book, surpassing the previous record of 34 held by *Jane Eyre*.

YOU MUST CHOOSE!

Risk-taking

Would you rather...

try to walk once around on the edge at the top of the Empire State Building on a windy day

OR

head-butt a Rottweiler 10 times and see what happens?

YOU MUST CHOOSE!

On a cross-country flight, would you rather sit next to...

a heavy breather **OR** a two-year-old?

an unshowered hobo **OR** a Mormon missionary?

an argumentative matador **OR** Gropey McGee?

ROADKILL THE ADJECTIVE PROFESSION GAME

One person randomly throws out a personality trait (somber, bashful, giddy, etc.). Another person randomly throws out a profession (baker, Driver's Ed instructor, accountant, etc.). Put them together (somber baker). A third person does a quick impression and improvisation of the newly created character. Hilarity ensues.

YOU MUST CHOOSE!

Would you rather...

take a fastball to the thigh from Roger Clemens

OR

take a kick in the nuts from the Indianapolis Colts' Adam Vinatieri?

YOU MUST CHOOSE!

You fail, you die.

If your life depended on it, would you rather...

stack three uncooked rice grains on top of each other

OR

spin three quarters at once?
Things to consider: Try it. You have five minutes.

If your life depended on it, would you rather...

have to achieve orgasm while listening to the soundtrack
to *The Wizard of Oz*

OR

while staring at a framed 8x10 photo of former
Surgeon General C. Everett Koop?
Things to consider: Try it. You have five minutes.

YOU MUST CHOOSE!

MILE 50:

LOST AND FOUND

Your brain is a blossoming azalea. Everything is alive. The traffic lights are winking at you, and the clouds are soaring Pegasi. Also, interestingly enough, it seems you've peed your pants. Or was it you? How can one be sure? Such is the path to Enlightenment: a certain ambiguity that slips through your fingers like a Porridge of Truth and stains your crotch like the Urine of Justice. The Deity's questions continue: Like a spiritual spotter, he urges you onward, yet not with command but with inquiry. You've just completed rep eight of set three of your divine workout, and you have left your spiritual sweat on the weight bench. Towel that off, asshole! The Deity's language of choice now consists of varying patterns of teeth-flossing, emanating the deep notes of a mournful cello. Your mind grazes free-range on the Deity's dental detritus. As the dilemmas get randomer, warpeder, and whackeder, you are lost. You are found. You are addicted to the nubile curves of the question mark.

Would your rather...

conclude all prayers with "Yeah Boyeeee!" instead of "Amen"

OR

have your family solemnly recite the lyrics to the "Super Bowl Shuffle" instead of the Lord's Prayer before each meal?

Things to consider: (say with very grave tone) "We are the Bears Shufflin' Crew; shufflin' on down, doin' it for you. We're so bad, we know we're good. Blowin' your mind like we knew we would. Yeah boyeeeee!"

YOU MUST CHOOSE!

Would you rather...

cough anally

OR

fart orally? Excrete ocularly?
Things to consider: getting bronchitis

Would you rather...

raise your child to think he/she's the reincarnation of Roy Rogers

OR

have your self-esteem entirely based on Meadowlark Lemmon's opinion of you?

YOU MUST CHOOSE!

Would you rather...

play *Guitar Hero* with Jimi Hendrix **OR** Slash?

Kurt Cobain **OR** John Denver?

Jimmy Page **OR** Abe Lincoln?

YOU MUST CHOOSE!

(Typo-inspired)
Would you rather...

have an incurable case of head dice

OR

get a face-shift (everything pulled a little to the left)?

Would you rather...

be able to speak English but only be able to hear words that are spoken to you in Uzbek

OR

have a corneal disease that causes you to not be able to see the letter "s"?

Things to consider: translators, the Slaughterhouse

YOU MUST CHOOSE!

Would you rather...

have thorn-covered skin

OR

at parties, be unable to hold conversations about anything other than Max Headroom?

Would you rather...

have to conduct all business meetings sitting in a *Pole Position* arcade game

OR

anytime you see a baguette, have an unstoppable compulsion to wield it and smash things maniacally like Bamm-Bamm from the *Flintstones*?

YOU MUST CHOOSE!

Would you rather...

be able to turn any piece of paper into a Post-it note

OR

be able to immediately end arguments if you sneeze?

YOU MUST CHOOSE!

Would you rather...

every Thursday, have a Samurai sword permanently but painlessly embedded in your back, causing you to stagger around, constantly about to die, forever trying to utter your last words

OR

gradually turn your surroundings into a Panera wherever you go starting after about 15 minutes and taking about an hour to completely Panera-ize?

YOU MUST CHOOSE!

Would you rather...

have your brain put on size and weight as you learn new things

OR

have everything sound as if your voice is trailing away as if you're falling off a cliff?

Things to consider: Would you just stay dumb?; reciting wedding vows

YOU MUST CHOOSE!

Would you rather...

have sexual hormone levels that vary with the performance of the New York Stock Exchange

OR

only be able to text the word "lozenge"?

YOU MUST CHOOSE!

Would you rather...

have a loyal hunting falcon at your beck and call but have perpetual hat head

OR

be able to pull off wearing tights but be shamefully attracted to Dora the Explora?

YOU MUST CHOOSE!

Would you rather...

be a world class platform diver but painfully envy elk

OR

be able to summarize things with just the right amount of detail but have a codependent relationship with a merman?

YOU MUST CHOOSE!

Would you rather...

be a world class pole-vaulter but be unable to resist eating Scrabble tiles

OR

never be able to grasp the concept of a baker's dozen, but be a genius in every other way?

Things to consider: getting bagels for the think tank

YOU MUST CHOOSE!

Would you rather...

have the navigational instincts of Amerigo Vespucci but subsist on a diet of pet food

OR

be able to shine shoes with your gaze but have to make love to a croissant on a daily basis?

YOU MUST CHOOSE!

Would you rather...

have to walk single file with your friends whenever you went anywhere, have your dreams directed by the guy who directed Pan's Labyrinth, be able to enter the water without making a splash, but uncontrollably exclaim names of the various members of the Continental Congress during sexual climax

OR

have literal cauliflower ear, have a herring for a left hand, have to name your child Aesop, constantly be framing shots with your hands like a director, turn guys named Mervin yellow, and be able to spit pools that show visions of the future for a peasant in Laos?

YOU MUST CHOOSE!

Would you rather...

have a cork back, a comb-over beard, lust after Puss in Boots, have Wes Unseld's shadow, play daily Arkanoid games with Tony Randall, have to *register for your wedding* at Spencers Gifts and have *basil-scented farts*

OR

have *butter-soaked skin*, a maple scone for a foot, get 5 o'clock *shadow all over your body*, have a *vast coaster* collection, have *Carl Weathers* borrow your pen and never *give it back*, and have a bulimia that causes you to want to *throw up* in mail slots?

YOU MUST CHOOSE!

Would you rather...

sneeze the sound of thunder

OR

pee pure energy?

YOU MUST CHOOSE!

T(HERE)?

You have heard "If you see the Buddha on the side of the Road, kill him." That is to say that the eternal journey *is* the destination, *that endless* asking is the answer. The trip is a Mobius strip highway, a toy race track, a motorized model choo choo infinity sign figure 8 on its side reel to reel flickering filmstrip exercise bike. The journey is over and *yet*, what is the end but the beginning from another direction? YOU CANNOT SPELL "THERE" WITHOUT "HERE." *Woops, you peed your pants* again.

Hope you had a nice trip. The great thing is, you can always hit the road again. Here are more games you can play during your next trip or the continuation of this one.

BELOW THE BELT

Whoever is reading must convey the words below using charades. But here's the catch. You can only use your body from the waist down. (Driver, keep your eyes on the road!)

Baseball ✌ Poop ✌ Pray ✌ Rocket ✌ Ejaculate ✌ Crabs

Shake ✌ Pendulum ✌ Athlete's Foot ✌ Croissant

Don't stop there. Have someone choose more words and whisper them to the actor.

PHOTO SCAVENGER HUNT — ROADKILL

See if you can get pictures of the following items during your trip. If you want, break into two teams. The team to get the most points by the end of the trip wins. Feel free to email your complete set of photos to princealbert@wouldyourather.com.

Items:

- Old discarded tire (1 point)
- Thing that holds six pack together, littered (1 point)
- Skid marks (1 point)
- A man with a nametag (weirdest name wins 5 points)
- Person giving the finger (1 point per picture)
- Mullet (5 points)
- Something undeniably depressing (5 points)
- Someone who looks vaguely like Jimmy Smits (10 points)
- Prince Albert piercing (50 points)
- Skeleton (50 points)

A Day at the Store

One day _____ and _____ went to the store. They

     person in room   *another person in room*

pulled out their _____ and bought a _____. Then they

             plural noun   *noun*

_____ ed to the _____ aisle. Once there, they murdered

  verb   *dictator*

a baby. They then sat on a blue goose. Later they made love to a

conch shell. Then they confessed they always dreamed of rapidly

taking a big washing machine on a sloppy green Jimmy Walker.

"_____" said Leonard.

  part of body

A TWIST ON A CLASSIC

Origins

In the beginning _____ created the heavens and the _____ . And
_{person}

the earth was without _____ , and _____ . And God said, Let there be
_{noun}

_____ : and there was light. And God saw the light, that it was _____.
_{noun}

And God called the light _____ , and the darkness he called _____ .
_{adjective}

And God made the firmament, and God called the firmament _____ .
_{Smurf}

And God said " _____ ": and it was so.
_{exclamation}

Blasphemer!

WHAT WOULD YOU BE...?

One person thinks of someone who everybody in the group knows: a friend, a coworker, an enemy, a teacher, etc. The player who is thinking of someone answers each question below as if he were that person. After the questions, have a player guess who you are thinking of.

If you were a bar drink or cocktail, what would you be?

If you were any character from a movie or TV show, who would you be?

If you were a Greek god, who would you be?

If you were a Beatle, which one would you be?

If you were a facial expression, what would you be? (Make it.)

You can also just ask the questions and answer for yourselves and friends.

If you like this game, there are lots more questions in *What Would You Be...?* at book stores and wouldyourather.com.

PORNIFICATION ROADKILL

Porn·i·fi·ca·tion:

noun, 1) the art of turning a legitimate movie title into a porno by manipulating a word or group of words in the title, often employing the use of puns to create a lurid, sexually suggestive title 2) a skill to make your parents proud

Take turns making up legit movie titles and pornifying them. Examples below:

Title	Pornification
The Nutty Professor	The Slutty Professor
Cold Mountain	Cold Mountin'
Malcolm X	Malcolm XXX
Space Jam	Face Jam
Analyze This	Analize This
Big Trouble in Little China	Big Trouble in Little Vagina

How many more can you think of? For more, check out pornifythis.com and the book *Pornification*.

Each player or team reads an Objectives Page (and does not look at the other Objectives Page). Read the objectives to yourself, making sure that no one else sees them. Now, go about your business as you normally would, looking for opportunities to achieve your objectives.

MIND CONTROL OBJECTIVES PAGE 1

Get an opponent to:

- Retrieve an item from the garbage.
- Draw the "Peace" symbol.
- Unbutton a button on another person's clothing.
- Say "radish" and "milk" in the same sentence.
- Say "nice shot."
- Put on another person's glasses.
- Imitate a farm animal.

All of the objectives require you to get one of your opponents to do something. It can be any one of your opponents, and not all opponents must be present when the objective is achieved. After you successfully achieve an objective and verbally reveal it to your opponent(s), reward yourself one point. The game is over when a player successfully scores three points.

MIND CONTROL OBJECTIVES PAGE 2

Get an opponent to:

- Say "You're/You are an idiot."
- Give the "thumbs-down" sign.
- Sing a line from a Beatles song.
- Perform a push-up.
- Say "plum" and "asparagus" in the same sentence.
- Put his/her own finger in his/her own ear.
- Clap.

Make up your own *Would you rather...?* questions, using the ideas below:

sushi roll	knuckles	Zork
Bilbo Baggins	Gas-Ex	metaphor
right angles	swimming cap	Rogaine
moat	the letter "N"	wheelchair
Cagney & Lacey	salt	spiral
Quickbooks	ankles	pendulum
rotten	Wasssssupppp!	mist
the concept of aging	anime	hieroglyph
Corona	migraines	boom mic
chipmunks	pork	bloody bowel movements
Rotterdam	Edmonton	Raggedy Ann & Andy

About The Authors

Justin Heimberg is a comedy writer who has written for all media including movies, TV, books, and magazines. He, along with David Gomberg, runs Falls Media, an entertainment company specializing in providing short and funny creative services and products.

David Gomberg is notably different from other oozes. Being a growth, he is fixed to one place and cannot move or attack. For the most part, he is forced to feed off of vegetable, organic or metallic substances in an underground wall. If he grows on a ceiling, however, he can sense if someone passes below, and drops onto them. Living creatures touched by Gomberg eventually turn into Gomberg themselves. Gomberg is vulnerable to light, heat, frost, and cure disease spells. Gomberg is mindless and cannot speak. As such, he is regarded as neutral in alignment. Gomberg will re-grow if even the tiniest residue remains, and can germinate to form a full sized ooze again years later.

Got Your Own Question?

Go to wouldyourather.com to submit questions and read hundreds of other absolutely absurd dilemmas.

More Books ✳ Original Comedy

Games and Calendars ✳ Discounts

Contests ✳ And/or More!

wouldyourather.com

About "Would You Rather...?" Books:

Us guys, the authors of the *Would You Rather...?* books, believe that the great joys in life are the times spent hanging out with your friends, laughing. Our books aim to facilitate that. They are Socially Interactive Humor Books. SIHB's. Damnit, that acronym sucks! Let's try again... Socially Interactive Games & Humor SIGH... exactly the opposite of what we are looking for in an abbreviation. Son of a bitch. Alright look, these books make you think in interesting ways and talk to your friends, and laugh and be funny. They are, and they make you, imaginative and irreverent. Lots of bang for your buck (and vice versa.) *WYR* books provide 3-300 hours of entertainment depending on how painfully retarded your reading pace is. So take these books, hang out with your friends, and have a good time.

Other *Would You Rather...?*® Books:

Would You Rather...?: Love & Sex asks you to ponder such questions as:

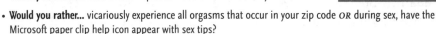

- **Would you rather...** orgasm once every ten years OR once every ten seconds?

- **Would you rather...** have to have sex in the same position every night OR have to have sex in a different position every night (you can never repeat)?

- **Would you rather...** have breast implants made of Nerf® OR Play-Doh®?

- **Would you rather...** vicariously experience all orgasms that occur in your zip code OR during sex, have the Microsoft paper clip help icon appear with sex tips?

Would You Rather...?: Love & Sex can be read alone or played together as a game.   Laugh-out-loud funny, uniquely imaginative, and deceptively thought-provoking, *Would You Rather...?: Love & Sex* is simultaneously the authors' most mature and immature work yet!

Would You Rather...? 2: Electric Boogaloo
Another collection of over three hundred absurd alternatives and demented dilemmas. Filled with wacky wit, irreverent humor and twisted pop-culture references.

Would You Rather...?: Pop Culture Edition
A brand new collection of deranged dilemmas and preposterous predicaments, featuring celebrities and trends from popular culture. Ponder and debate questions like: *Would you rather... be machine-gunned to death with Lite-Brite pegs or be assassinated by Cabbage Patch Dolls?*

Would You Rather...?: Illustrated — Tired of having to visualize these dilemmas yourself? No need anymore with this book of masterfully illustrated ***Would You Rather...?*** dilemmas. Now you can see what it looks like to be attacked by hundreds of Pilsbury Doughboys, get hole-punched to death, sweat cheese, or have pubic hair that grows an inch every second. A feast for the eyes and imagination, ***Would You Rather...?: Illustrated*** gives Salvador Dali a run for his money.

Would You Rather...?'s What Would You Be?
Stretch your metaphor muscles along with your imagination as you answer and discuss thought/humor-provoking questions like: If you were a Smurf, which one would you be? What if you were a type of dog? A road sign? A Beatle? A nonsense sound?

wouldyourather.com
falls-media.com
classlesseducation.com

Would You Rather...?'s What's Your Price?
Would you punch your grandmother in the stomach as hard as you can for $500,000?
There are no wrong answers but hundreds of "wrong" questions in an irresistibly irreverent book.

Would You Rather...? for Kids
The first book in the series written and designed for kids ages 8 and older, *Would You Rather...? for Kids* features hundreds of devilish dilemmas and imaginative illustrations! Kids will crack up as they ponder questions such as: **Would you rather...** have a tape-dispensing mouth OR a bottle opening nostril?

Also by Falls Media

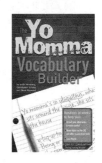

The Yo Momma Vocabulary Builder
Increasing word power sounds like one of those dreary chores best pawned off on somebody else. *The Yo Momma Vocabulary Builder*, the first in Falls Media's series of irreverent, educational books, makes the activity not only endurable but irresistible. The authors use classic dissing and one-upsmanship to slyly introduce a wide range of words.

More Books by Falls Media

The Official Movie Plot Generator

"A Coffee Table Masterpiece" - *Newsweek*.

The Official Movie Plot Generator is a unique and interactive humor book that offers 27,000 hilarious movie plot possibilities you create, spanning every genre of cinema from feel-good family fun to hard-boiled crime drama to soft-core pornography. Just flip the book's ninety tabs until you find a plot combination you like. For movie fans or anyone who likes to laugh a lot with little effort, *The Official Movie Plot Generator* is a perfect gift and an irresistible, offbeat diversion.

Pornification

"For every legit movie, there exists (at least theoretically), a porn version of that movie." *Pornification* includes over 500 "pornified" titles, along with hysterical quizzes, games and challenges. There's something for everyone, from *Cold Mountin'* to *The Fast and Bicurious* to *Malcolm XXX*, so open up and enjoy!

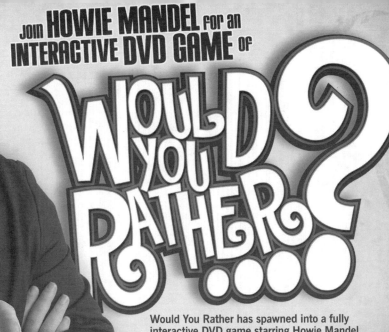

JOIN **HOWIE MANDEL** FOR AN
INTERACTIVE DVD GAME OF

WOULD YOU RATHER...?

Would You Rather has spawned into a fully
interactive DVD game starring Howie Mandel.
Check it out at all leading retailers or visit
www.imaginationgames.com

TOYS Я US   ✷ Imagination.

It's time to take a trip to the realm of the Absurd and expand your mind with some inanely insightful inquiry...

Would you rather...
live in a world comprised of Lego

OR

Play-Doh?

Would you rather...
have a bad acid trip in Amish Country

OR

in Bed Bath & Beyond?

Would you rather...
impulsively perform ten wild pelvic thrusts every hour on the hour

OR

be unable to refrain from "sacking" the elderly as soon as you see them?

WYR Trippin' has more than just deranged dilemmas.
It's also full of all-new hilarious games perfect for the road, room, and soul!